George Rosie

Cromarty
the scramble for oil

D1437503

CANONGATE
Edinburgh

Published by
Canongate Publishing, Ltd.
17 Jeffrey Street
Edinburgh

Photographs by Graham Metcalfe
Cover design by James Hutcheson

ISBN 0 903937 05 0

Printed in Great Britain by
Paramount Printers, Edinburgh

Introduction

The oil industry is probably the best thing to happen to Scotland, and especially northern Scotland, for many years. A depressed region is suddenly revitalised, given new hope. Among the ills it will help to eradicate are unemployment and low wages in an area where these have for too long been accepted as facts of life.

But it is important to notice mistakes, and to draw attention to the abuses, bad planning, lack of planning, exploitation and undue haste which so frequently bedevil enterprises of this sort. The Cromarty Firth is a useful example of the way in which massive oil development can create dissention in a community and transform the way of life of a whole area.

There are clear lessons in Easter Ross for the rest of Scotland, especially for those areas which are likely to be affected by the arrival of the oil men. In the main they are the problems of an area which has been shaken into life. There is much in Easter Ross to be concerned about, and much to be thankful for.

George Rosie.

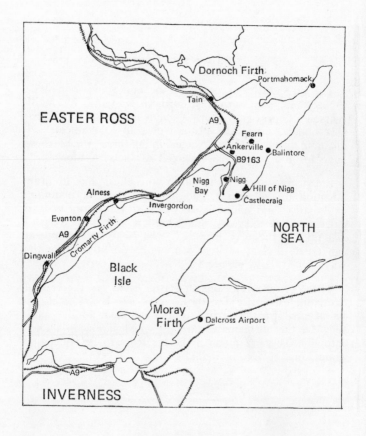

The Cromarty Firth

1

The May 1970 local elections in Ross and Cromarty were an interesting business. After years of rumour, speculation, gossip, hope, and aborted plans, it was beginning to look as if big industry was on its way to the Cromarty Firth. British Aluminium (a subsidiary of the American-owned Reynolds Aluminium) were building their smelter at Invergordon; hundreds of acres had been re-zoned for industrial use, development companies had been sniffing around and buying up land, and plans were being floated for petrochemical works, tanker terminals, tank farms and even an oil refinery. There was also the prospect — and it was becoming clearer by the week — of spin-off from the oilfields being discovered off the coast. The election was fought on the issue of whether it should be allowed to happen.

At the north end of the Cromarty Firth around the district of Nigg, a particularly fierce little electoral battle was waged in 1970. The local councillor, Marjorie Linklater (wife of novelist Eric Linklater), had retired, and John Robertson of Castlecraig Farm, an enthusiastic supporter of industry and industrialisation, was running a campaign which claimed that "the time for industry is now". His opponent was his sister Anne, wife of his neighbour Robert Hunter Gordon of Pitcalzean Mains farm.

Anne Hunter Gordon insists that she was not opposed to development *per se,* but "felt that it should be well-sited, if possible preserving good agricultural land; it should have good financial backing, and the amenity of the local people should be preserved." (She did, however, make a formal objection to the proposal by a firm called Grampian Chemicals to develop about 600 acres of agricultural land at Delny, near Invergordon.)

"Interesting elections those," John Robertson recalls. "Very much a pro-development or anti-development affair. But the 'antis' — the people who wanted to stop the industry — were very much the upper middle class, especially the ones who had moved into the area after the war. There was a lot of 'For God's sake don't let's make servants too expensive' kind of talk at the time . . ."

But while the local gentry were reeling back, appalled, most of the people of Easter Ross felt otherwise. The area — like the rest of Scotland, especially northern Scotland — has a sour history of poverty, unemployment, lack of opportunity and emigration. So when the chance came they voted for jobs. "The voting was very decisive," claims Robertson, "I would say 2-1 to 4-1 in favour of the 'development' candidates."

Some people are prepared to dispute these statistics, but whatever the precise figures were, John Robertson was the new councillor for the Nigg district. Anne Hunter Gordon was left to carry on her campaign as best she could, trying to lessen the impact of the developments when they could not be stopped, insisting that local people should be given as much information as possible about the developments that affected their lives, and generally making life difficult for the developers.

John Robertson, as he freely admits, is not a disinterested party. He has made a great deal of money from the industrial potential of the Cromarty Firth. In 1968 he sold off 220 acres of his dairy farm to an industrial developer for £140,000.

But ironically the Hunter Gordons, who have gone to some length to resist the encroachment of industrialisation around the Hill of Nigg, have made a great deal more money. In 1972 Hunter Gordon sold seventeen acres of poor quality duneland to Ken Armstrong of Oilfield Supplies for nearly £18,000. (This was a good price, but Armstrong resold the land for a very handsome profit.)

When it became clear that the industrialists could not be stopped (and that the council had re-zoned most of his farm for industrial use), Hunter Gordon bowed to the inevitable and sold the remaining 600 acres of Pitcalzean Mains farm to the Cromarty Firth Development Company for over £1 million. To his credit, Hunter Gordon did insist on a series of conditions to the sale: the protection of the interests of seventeen nearby householders, the protection and maintenance of the old parish church, the recording of the site of Dunskeath Castle, and early consultation with the Nature Conservancy.

The Hunter Gordons have now moved to the more pastoral climate of Angus, having bought an upland arable and stock farm at Overfinlarg.

This is an example of the kind of thing that happens, the kind of money that changes hands, and the kind of inter-communal (and inter-family) disputes which break out when competition for prime industrial land becomes fierce. And of all the rural areas of Scotland affected by the drive for oil, the land around the deepwater anchorage of the Cromarty Firth has been the most sought after, the most hotly disputed and, perhaps, the most deeply transformed.

2

The Cromarty Firth (as the British Navy well knew) had a great deal to offer: a superb anchorage, sheltered from the full blast of the east wind by the high Sutors of Cromarty; a deepwater channel running miles back into the Firth; decent road and railway communications, and, most important, a series of flat peninsulas jutting out into the Firth, consisting of scrubland and reclaimable sand. All of this lay within easy towing distance of the major North Sea oilfields.

Not surprisingly, the oilfield supply companies and the big construction firms seeking to break into platform building moved fast. Within a couple of years almost every decent site on the Cromarty Firth had been snapped up by the big operators. Land which for generations had belonged to local gentry, farmers and distilleries, suddenly passed into the hands of a tangle of international companies based in London, Edinburgh, Italy, Idaho, Houston, or New York. It was an amazingly rapid build-up of industry, geared to the needs of the men working the North Sea oilfields.

One of the sites to change hands was on the Evanton peninsula, where in June 1973 Mr Munro of Balconie Farm sold 143 acres of mixed farmland for £135,000 to a firm calling themselves Brital Marine Construction. At that stage a number of companies were involved (although not formally) with Brital Marine — Richard Dunstan, the Hull shipbuilders, and three three Italian engineering firms, Micoperi, Saipem and Interconsult.

With that kind of backing the council had little hesitation about giving Brital Marine planning permission to "construct offshore structures" on the site at Evanton. But for reasons which are still not clear, Richard Dunstan and the three Italian companies then dropped out of the association. According to the biggest of the Italian firms, Saipem, they "had early discussions with Brital Marine Construction but that was all. I can assure you that Saipem no longer has any involvement with this company." Micoperi tell the same story.

As far as can be ascertained, Brital Marine made no bids for the production platform contracts, and no work was ever started on the site. Despite repeated attempts by Ross and Cromarty County Council to contact the firm, no reply was forthcoming. "It really was a one-sided correspondence," says Gwyn Davies, the Ross and Cromarty development officer. No letters were answered and no telephone calls were returned.

But in 1974 the 143 acres of the site were placed for sale (with planning permission) with the Edinburgh office of Knight, Frank & Rutley. The price quoted was £2,000 an acre, and "negotiations are taking place." If the deal goes through at that price, Brital Marine Construction stand to make more than £150,000 profit, having held the land for one year.

On the same little peninsula, on the other side of the river Graad, lay a stretch of land belonging to Arthur Brocklehurst Luttrell Munro-Ferguson, laird of Novar, owner of the Novar estates, and one of the wealthiest and most enterprising landowners in the north of Scotland. His patch was interesting: it was flat, and only yards away from the Cromarty Firth deepwater channel. It also included a wartime airfield with a complex of old buildings. It was a prime site, and Munro-Ferguson knew it.

In June 1972 the laird of Novar joined a firm called the Evanton Development Co., set up a few months previously by Sir William Lithgow of the famous Clydeside ship-building family. The conjunction of Munro-Ferguson's land and Lithgow's engineering expertise was to prove profitable. In March 1973 the Evanton Development Co. was bought into by a Houston financing operation called Highland Resources Inc. Two new directors appeared on the list, Clyde Jones of Houston, and Ralph Sturgis O'Connor, also of Houston. (O'Connor, as it happens, is son-in-law of George Brown, a director of Highland Resources and Chairman of Brown and Root, the engineering firm.)

The name of the company was changed to Highland Deephaven, and in the middle of 1973 Munro-Ferguson sold the site to the company for £836,900. The company then set up office in Inverness, and hired Bob Kilpatrick, one of Ross and Cromarty's most energetic officers. Since then it has been pushing large and ambitious plans for a deepwater port, storage and an industrial site.

A few miles further north there is a similar little peninsula which juts out into the Firth near the village of Alness. Its characteristics are almost identical: flat land (even an airfield), a sandy beach, road and rail links, and easy access to the deepwater channel. Like the Evanton peninsula, the area is neatly bisected by a small river.

The land south of the river Alness was snapped up by the giant building/engineering contractor Taylor Woodrow. In June 1972 they lodged an application with Ross and Cromarty County Council for outline approval of "facilities for the construction of structures for sub-sequent installation offshore" or, in other words, concrete production platforms. Within a few months, they had their outline permission.

By the summer of 1974 not one turf had been turned on the site, but Taylor Woodrow have high hopes. They are currently tendering for platforms, and have a good chance of winning the contract for the Mobil platform for the Beryl field. They have also recently received detailed permission for their yard.

The site on the other side of the river Alness was collared in 1972 by an American supply and service company called Mid-Continent Supply, who lodged an almost identical application. As soon as they had their land, Mid-Continent sought and obtained permission for yet another concrete platform site. After a hiatus of about a year Mid-Continent leased the site (or at least part of it) to a British/French/Danish consortium led by the large Surrey firm of Peter Lind.

But Mid-Continent have not done a straightforward landlord/tenant deal. They make it quite clear that they are still very interested in what goes on at Alness, and have written in conditions which ensure themselves a slice of the action as and when the Lind consortium get a platform to build. "We're very interested in providing the gear that goes on top of the platform," they explain, "rather than building the platform itself."

But according to Kiers, the other British firm in the Lind consortium, there is a chance that the site may never get off the ground. After citing the problems — housing, labour, transport costs, etc — Kiers came to the conclusion that " it really is remarkably difficult to build anything up there — and at least 10-15% more expensive". The company make it quite clear that if the consortium could find a similar site with all the right conditions further south, they would jump at it. "But we have nowhere in mind," they add. The Cromarty Firth's combination of proximity to the oilfields, and a deepwater channel, are hard to beat.

If the two yards ever do get under way, Alness will be swamped. Kiers, for one, admit the problem of "overloading the facilities". "And our yard will be quite small: no more than 300 men. Taylor Woodrow have much more ambitious plans, to employ at least 600 men, maybe more." This would leave the council with a staggering series of problems: not least the appalling prospect of lorry after lorry trailing aggregate sand and reinforcing steel through the village of Alness (which is on the A9). The council want Taylor Woodrow and the Scottish Office to get together and finance a by-pass south of Alness, with an access road to the site.

A few miles up the A9 at Saltburn near Invergordon, oil-related industry is in full swing. In 1972 an Anglo-American firm called MK-Shand moved into the area, and began operating a 50 acre site which they held on a 15 year lease from the British Aluminium Co. MK-Shand was formed early in 1971 as a pipe construction operation. They were 75% owned by Morrison-Knudsen of Boise, Idaho, and 25% by the British Shand group.

But the big demand was not so much for pipe construction as for putting concrete wrappings on steel pipe destined for the bottom of the North Sea. MK-Shand moved fast, bringing in a Dutch firm which had pipe-coating experience, found their site ("We searched all along the east coast for flat land and deep water") and started work at Invergordon, where "the local authorities were very helpful".

Within months they had the order to put concrete wraps on the submarine pipeline which BP were running from their Forties Field to Cruden Bay. "We've finished that now," they say. "All we have to do now is handle it from the jetty on to the ships."

The next big order was not long in coming. In 1973 MK-Shand were given the job of coating the 230 miles of subsea pipe being laid by the French firm Total from their Frigg gas field to St. Fergus near Peterhead. Last year, to keep up with their work, MK-Shand extended their yard by another 30 acres, giving them 80 acres altogether.

It was quite a build-up. In the space of a few years an economy which had coasted along very modestly on a mixture of farming, the aluminium smelter, some light industry and small-scale navy servicing, had been transformed. Hotels in Dingwall, Invergordon, Tain, Balintore, and Evanton were suddenly frequented by some of the sharpest business heads in Europe, competing with each other for the best sites, the best conditions and the best options around. The quiet backwater of the Cromarty Firth had moved into the centre of a massive economic and industrial game which was being controlled in Houston, London, Paris and Milan.

3

If there is one enterprise which can be said to have transformed the face of the Cromarty Firth, it is the yard set up by Highland Fabricators, down on Nigg point at the entrance to the Firth. Tucked in the lee of the Hill of Nigg, and built on a few hundred acres of reconstituted dune-land, scrub and reclaimed beach, the yard was designed to build the huge steel production platforms needed to extract the oil from the North Sea. For sheer impact — economic, social, industrial, political — none of the other oil-generated projects in Easter Ross can compare with the Highland Fabricators' platform-building yard.

As the oil companies never tire of reminding everyone, extracting oil from the North Sea is no easy business. When BP struck it rich with their "Forties" field, they were faced with the daunting prospect of getting it out from under 450 feet of water. This meant ordering massive production platforms, the biggest ever built, structures capable of withstanding the atrocious weather of the northern North Sea with its huge waves, ice and snap hurricanes. There were very few companies in the world capable of the undertaking. After months of discussion, agonising and research the job went to the Houston based engineering firm of Brown and Root.

The Brown and Root designers came back with an impressive piece of technology. What was needed, they said, was a set of four huge steel structures, each about 550 feet high (more than 700 feet to the top of the drilling derricks). Each platform was to consist of a support structure (jacket) consisting of 20,000 tons of steel, topped by a 3,000 ton deck, 12,000 tons of well casing, 13,000 tons of machinery, piping, etc, to be transfixed hundreds of feet into the sea bed with 9,000 tons of steel piling. The whole package would weigh 57,000 tons, and each would cost roughly £50 million. The platforms would be linked to one another by a submarine pipeline, which would then run 110 miles to Cruden Bay in Aberdeenshire, and from there overland to a specially built tanker terminal at Grangemouth.

It was quite a scheme, and far too big for one firm, no matter how large and experienced. BP gave Brown and Root three separate contracts: one to design and supervise all four platforms, one to build the support structures or jackets for two of the platforms, and another to lay half the submarine pipeline.

With structures of that size and weight, Brown and Root reasoned, the nearer the oilfields the better. So

14

after scouring most of Europe and North Africa for sites, they finally opted for a yard on the Cromarty Firth (much to the delight of the regional and local authorities). The yard that Brown and Root needed to build involved a massive amount of fairly sophisticated civil engineering — site clearance, reclamation, dock building, flood gates etc. For a variety of reasons, not the least of which were political, it was decided to go in with a British company.

At the end of 1971 a new company was registered in Edinburgh, called Highland Fabricators. Despite its name, Highland Fabricators was not a Scottish concern. The company is a consortium, with Brown and Root of Houston the senior partner, owning $66\frac{2}{3}\%$. The junior partner, with $33\frac{1}{3}\%$, is George Wimpey (although Wimpey are about to increase their shareholding). The Chairman of Highland Fabricators is Sir Philip Southwell, Chairman of Brown and Root UK, and one of Britain's most experienced oil industry operators.

Brown and Root are a formidable concern. From their sprawling headquarters at 4,100 Clinton Drive, Houston, their chairman, George Brown, and his chief executive, Herbert Frensley, control an international work force of around 30,000 people. The company build almost anything, almost anywhere: hydro-electric dams in Montana and South Dakota, polythene plants in Australia and India, ports and harbours in Spain, Brazil, Ireland, Okinawa, Iran and Venezuela. Power stations, chemical plant, steelworks, highways, bridges, submarine pipeline, tunnels, mines and offshore drilling platforms — all are grist to Brown and Root's mill. Since their beginning more than fifty years ago as a fairly modest road-building partnership, Brown and Root have burgeoned into one of the biggest, most resourceful and most thrusting engineering construction firms in the world.

The company have a knack of involving themselves

in spectacular and often controversial engineering projects. There was, for example, the (now abandoned) Mohole project — a plan to pierce the earth's crust, by drilling through the ocean bed, to sample the hot interior. After much jockeying betwen half a dozen big firms, Brown and Root won the drilling contract (with the support, it was rumoured, of the late Lyndon Johnson, a politician much favoured by the Brown and Root hierarchy in Texas).

Over the years Brown and Root built up a great deal of expertise in building airfields and other installations for the military. The huge Guam complex was theirs. They were also involved in building NATO bases in France, and in the massive USAF and US Navy bases in Spain. They also did very well out of the Vietnam war. As part of the RMK-BRJ four-company consortium, they built most of the big military installations and airfields in South Vietnam. (The driving force behind the RMK-BRJ consortium was Morrison-Knudsen of Boise, Idaho — Morrison-Knudsen are 75% shareholders and the MK in MK-Shand, who have the pipe-coating yard at Invergordon.)

One of Brown and Root's most controversial projects was in Peru, a plan to drive a 146 mile highway through the Andes between Tarapato and Rio Nieva. Brown and Root designed the road and were given the job of overseeing the work on behalf of the Peruvian government. The actual construction work was to be carried out by Brown and Root's old associates, Morrison-Knudsen.

The work went badly. Particularly trying were the landslides which kept charging down the mountainsides, burying the new road and leaving Morrison-Knudsen with the expensive business of clearing up. Accusations began to fly about that Morrison-Knudsen had blundered and were responsible. Morrison-Knudsen protested hotly, and blamed the "geological instability" of the region. The Peruvian government, backed up by the Brown and Root engineer on the spot, refused to cough up the extra three million dollars that Morrison-Knudsen were demanding.

In September 1968, the top brass from Brown and Root and Morrison-Knudsen put their heads together. The meeting ended with Brown and Root changing their minds, over-ruling their engineer on the spot and awarding 2.2 million extra dollars to Morrison-Knudsen, their partners in Vietnam. The connection was not lost on the Peruvian government, which was outraged and slapped conspiracy and collusion suits on both companies. The Peruvian army took over, the dollars dried up, the road petered out and, according to the New York Times, "the people stayed on their mules and on their feet".

Large and powerful as they are, Brown and Root Inc. are merely a sizeable cog in a smoothly meshing machine called the Halliburton Company, which is the biggest oilfield supply company in the world. Based in Dallas, Texas, the company employs more than 54,000 people through a string of companies which make up the Halliburton conglomerate. Halliburton companies now operating in Scotland include Halliburton Services (equipment), Imco (drilling muds), Jet Research Center (explosives), Taylor Diving (deep-sea diving service), Jackson Marine (supply vessels), and, of course, Brown and Root. According to Mr Moriarty, who runs the Halliburton North Sea operation, "we all operate as separate identities", but overall control rests firmly with the Halliburton board in Dallas (which until recently included Governor John B. Connally — Nixon's ex-Treasury Secretary).

The Halliburton man in charge of the Nigg Yard is a Brown and Root vice-president called Herbert A. Nelson. Nelson is almost a caricature of the energetic western

American businessman: he fixes visitors with a friendly grin, a casual greeting and a hearty handshake, and is immediately on first name terms. He has silvery hair, heavy glasses; he wears dapper clothes, sports elaborately tooled high-heeled boots, and puffs incessantly at Camel cigarettes. He also claims to have the only air-conditioned office north of Inverness. For all his winning ways, Nelson is clearly sharp, fast and determined. "I'm the company V-P in charge of Europe and Africa," he explains. "I've been with them about ten years; worked in the States, Alaska, the Middle East, Africa . . ."

Every scrap of Herb Nelson's expertise and drive were needed to get the Forties project under way. But Highland Fabricators got off to a flying start. Within weeks of the company being formed the Wimpey men were on the site reclaiming it from the sand flats and duneland around Nigg Bay. It was a big job and it needed a lot of land. The company began to buy up as much of the surrounding property as they needed.

After a fast spending jag, Highland Fabricators found themselves owners of one small estate, plus fifteen houses and cottages. (Ironically the cottages which passed into Halliburton hands had names like Pleasant Cottage, Rose Cottage, Briar Cottage, Honeysuckle Cottage, Ivy Cottage . . .) On a distinctly larger scale the company paid £110,000 to novelist Eric Linklater for his Pitcalzean House and its attached 150 acres. Linklater has now moved to Aberdeenshire, and Brown and Root use the house as a VIP guest house and club.

By the middle of 1972 Highland Fabricators had almost completed what was being widely billed as "the biggest hole in Europe", the graving dock in which the steel jackets would be built. It was an extraordinarily rapid build-up of a vast site in a very isolated area. The huge graving dock (1,000 ft by 600 ft by 50 ft deep) is situated at the south end of the site, where the huge concrete dock gates open out into the deepwater channel at the entrance to the Firth. Adjacent to the dock is the quay through which heavy materials are shipped in (and through which small structures are shipped out).

To the north lies the complex of buildings which the site needs — the prefabrication shops, shot-blast and painting shop, pipe-rolling mill, plus offices, canteen, warehouses, car parking etc. According to Highland Fabricators, "expert landscaping architects" were brought in to landscape the site, hence the 1,600 saplings which have been planted (fairly meaningless, given the height of the huge sheds, not to mention the size of the structures which will be built in the dock).

The result, however, is a fairly spectacular sight. The yard became such a popular Sunday afternoon visit with the local population that Highland Fabricators put up a viewing platform on the road outside. This has since been taken away. "It was not safe," say the company. (But according to one of their gatekeepers an awful lot of telephoto lenses were being used from the platform.)

By the end of 1972, Highland Fabricators had more than 600 men working on the site. More than 77% of these men were described as "locals", but to the company a local is "anyone coming from north of the Caledonian canal". Thus an Orcadian, or a Lewisman, or even a Shetlander — who might take days to get to Nigg bay — all are described as locals. But there is no doubt that the yard was a sudden and very real drain on industries in the area. Farming, fishing and forestry provided about 10% of the labour force; the local electrical and electronic industry provided 7%; engineering 15%; woodworkers 2% transport industry $4\frac{1}{2}$%; and, perhaps most important, more than 11% of the Highland Fabricators' labour force was drawn out of the local construction industry, which meant that housebuilding and house repair were drastically curtailed (a fact that was to give Highland Fabricators some grief).

By the middle of 1973, the company were employing more than 1,300 workers and the figure was still rising, and the men were coming from further and further afield. As the supply of men from Easter Ross, Sutherland, Lewis, Caithness and the Orkneys began to dry up, men were brought in from the Clyde, central Scotland, then Tyneside, Lancashire, London and South Wales. There were even (not very successful) attempts to attract skilled welders from Holland, France and Germany. "They'd bring in the Eskimos if they thought it would help," was one sour comment on recruiting policy.

At the beginning of 1974 the workforce numbered more than 1,500. The company said they expected it to climb to 1,750, a peak, and then settle back to 1,200. By midsummer the figure had reached 2,000 in a drive to get the Forties Field platform out before the winter.

For some time now the Highland Fabricators' yard has been touted as the "Klondike" of the north of Scotland, and the countryside and towns are full of rumours about the vast sums of money being paid to anyone prepared to walk through the gate and pick up a welding torch. In fact the wages are not enormous. The basic rate for a skilled tradesman — a welder, say, or a fabricator — was, until recently, 91p an hour, or £36 for a forty hour week. There is however plenty of overtime, and most men (after working a sixty hour week) take home between £50 and £60 after tax.

But while the local people may be satisfied with the rates, the men from the south are not. "I came here because I lost my job in Glasgow," one welder said, "but I'll be back like a shot when I can. This money is rubbish, for the work you do: I don't think they'd get

21

away with it south of Inverness. I'm bloody sure they wouldn't get away with it in England." His view is confirmed by a Wimpey man: "I was earning a hell of a lot more than this building platforms in England for the natural gas fields — a quid an hour at least, and that was seven years ago."

On top of their wages most of the men are paid "condition money". This varies from 2p an hour for working in mud, to 5p an hour for wearing an air mask, and 12p an hour heat money for working inside the big pipes. "Look at that," said a scaffolder, pointing to his condition money sheet, "7p an hour for working between 100 and 200 feet, and 10p an hour for working over 200 feet. As if it made any difference if you fell . . ."

The dominant grouse among the men working at Nigg is not so much the money as the working conditions. There is an endless stream of complaints from welders, riggers, scaffolders, fabricators, and labourers, about conditions in the yard.

The bitterest complaints of all come from the welders who have to work inside the large diameter pipes. "I'd like to see the doctors round here produce a figure for the number of sore throats they treat," said one welder. "We're inside the bloody pipes, breathing fumes all the time. When you spit it comes out black, pitch black: I'm not surprised the absenteeism is terrible in the yard. They blame their turnover on bad housing, but I'm not so sure. If a man wants a house or a deposit on a caravan, he works all the hours he can get to put away some money. That's what he will do normally. Not take days off, or get on the train . . ."

The welders' complaints were borne out by a report prepared for the firm by the Scottish Occupation Health Laboratory Service, who looked into the conditions in which the welders worked. The report, marked "Highly confidential to client", took the firm to task in no uncertain manner. "All of the welding operations," it said, "gave potentially hazardous concentration of one or other fume constituent of the plume rising from the weld." Arca air-welding gouging, a widely used process at Nigg, was said to create the risk of "excessive accumulation of iron oxide in the lungs; lung damage from oxides of nitrogen; metal fume fever from copper and excessive exposure to carbon monoxide. Acute irritation of the eyes and upper respiratory tract would also be caused . . ."

In general the report recommended that the firm either drastically improve the ventilation in the tanks, supply the men with "fresh air supplied positive pressure respirator", or make sure they work fewer hours in the prevailing conditions. Even the dust respirators issued to welders were found to be inadequate — "not likely to be effective against other fume constituents, in particular carbon monoxide".

The report went on to recommend routine health checks in three ways:

(a) Check for over-exposure to lead, manganese, copper and zinc by taking blood or urine samples.

(b) Check for over-exposure to iron oxide fume and possibly oxides of nitrogen by medical examination and chest x-ray.

(c) Check for over-exposure to carbon monoxide by taking blood samples for carboxyhaemoglobin determination or by measuring carbon monoxide in expired air.

According to the company, "all the recommendations on the report have been carried out." According to Paul Stafford, convenor of the shop stewards at the site, none of them have, "although they did bring up an x-ray van just before Christmas. But they were only here two days.

Fewer than 50% of the welders managed to get an x-ray, and none of the other trades. I don't see any sign of any real improvement in the conditions."

The combination of a largely unskilled labour force working at great speed, on a remote site in difficult working conditions, in a new industry, on the frontiers of technology, under foreign supervision, creates problems, to say the least. Highland Fabricators' policy has been to train their own work force of welders, riggers, scaffolders, fabricators etc, with a series of crash courses. Herb Nelson claims that the policy is working. "We're well pleased with our trainees," he says. "For green troops they're doing just fine." His view is not shared by many of the time-served tradesmen. "The locals," said one Glaswegian, "couldn't weld the crust on a pie. But how can you expect them to? You can't shove a man through a six week training course and expect him to come out the other end a welder. It's a skilled trade."

Others confirm this opinion. Myron D. Stepath, President of the Arcair Co., who make equipment for gouging out badly made or faulty welds, said in Inverness: "I took a trip to Scotland just to see what the hell Brown and Root were doing ordering so many of my machines." A Lousiana man, whose job was to x-ray the welds, thought that up to 30% or 40% were failures and had to be redone.

Riggers, fabricators and scaffolders were of the same opinion. "What can a lad learn in two or three weeks?" complained an experienced scaffolder. "I spent *three years* just watching and helping before they would let me one foot above the ground. But the lads here: they're expected to learn the job as they go along." A welder, who will have to work on the scaffolding that the scaffolders erect, shared these reservations. "I don't think the boys they train here will have the nerve, let alone

24

the ability, to go up 200 or 300 feet. You cannot make a man a scaffolder in two or three weeks. It's not on."

None of this makes for a happy work force. One way or another there are strong undercurrents of discontent and resentment. From time to time they flare up into walk-outs, strikes, picketing and working to rule. Much of this is specific, but quite a lot of the discontent seems to come from the inexperienced Americans rubbing the men (especially the skilled union men) up the wrong way.

The yard is more or less completely unionised, mainly by the Amalgamated Union of Engineering Workers and the Boilermakers Society, but Brown and Root, elsewhere in the world, do not recognise or work with trade unions. "The yanks," said one steward, "have never had to deal with unions in their life. Most of them don't see why they should have to start now." Paul Stafford, the convenor, tends to agree. "They have a way of fighting every little point. Getting them to concede anything is like trying to drag a drunk away from the bar. I'm the full-time convenor here, but I find myself being dragged into every little dispute that the stewards should be able to deal with — things that should never come to me."

There are also feelings that the Americans are forming a *de facto* ceiling, through which it is almost impossible for a Scot to rise. The official company policy is to replace the American foremen, overseers and managers with British people. "But that's just not happening," a steward complained. "There seem to be more yanks than ever. We're just not getting anywhere."

It may be that one of the reasons Brown and Root were attracted to the north of Scotland was the shortage and weakness of organised labour. The prospect of building the same kind of operation in, say, the Clyde, can hardly be expected to appeal to hard-headed American contractors. They were prepared to put up with all the disadvantages of a remote site rather than face the problems of recalcitrant labour.

The irony is that, thanks to the shortage of skilled men, they have been obliged to import some of the toughest union men in Britain, as well as having to cope with the problems of being in the far north. Officially the company say they would prefer to have only one union to deal with, but Herb Nelson does not seem too unhappy about dealing with several. "What's the old saw?" he reflected. "United they stand . . ."

Not surprisingly, Highland Fabricators fell behind their schedule. The original "float out" date for the Forties Field jacket was mid-1973. The target was then changed to the spring of 1974, later to July 1974. The race was on to get the structure out before the autumn gales made it impossible.

"I don't know if we'll get it out in time," said Herb Nelson. "We should do. We have a weather window of April to August: that's the only period the weather will be good enough. If we miss that . . . then we wait till spring next year." Part of the problem, as Nelson sees it, is that "we're working at the frontiers of technology. We're in production while we're still trying to design the things, developing new techniques as we go along."

All through the summer Highland Fabricators were crashing along on a critical path plan divided into ten-day sections. They injected more than £1 million in bonus money in a desperate effort to meet their "float out" date and get the platform in position before the weather broke. "If things go smoothly we should make it," said Paul Stafford. Some of his stewards (and many of the pundits) were not so confident, but the platform was eventually floated out on 17 August.

There is a certain irony when a big, powerful American company like Brown and Root move into an area like

26

Nigg. Under the Industry Act of 1972, Scotland is a development area. This means that *as of right* Highland Fabricators are entitled to claim back 20% of the cost of clearing their site, 20% of the cost of their buildings, and 20% of their capital equipment — most of which is bought in the U.S.A. That is not all: by way of tax allowance, 44% of their building costs are written off the first year, and 100% of the cost of their plant and equipment. Also for every man they train — and they are training men as fast as they can lay hands on them — the Department of Employment pays them £15 per week. All that, plus a few odds and ends like the Regional Employment Premium, adds up to what one American called "a great bunch of incentives," not the kind that Highland Fabricators are likely to lose out on. "I guess it's worth about £5 million to us," says Herb Nelson, "maybe more."

The big production platforms now due for installation on the Forties Field are being hailed as wonders of British technology and enterprise. They are hardly that: all four Forties field platforms were designed and are being supervised by Brown and Root, an American company, and two of the platforms are actually being built by Brown and Root. The thousands of tons of steel which are being used to build the platforms come mostly from Japan, France and Scandinavia. Five of the ten deck modules which will go on top of the platforms are being built in Holland. Most of the drilling equipment will come from America, and all the steel for the submarine pipeline will come from Japan. It will be coated by an American firm and laid under the sea by an American firm, Brown and Root, with an Italian firm, Saipem.

The great oil rush has more than just social and environmental disadvantages.

4

The speed at which the Highland Fabricators' yard was built up — from zero to more than 2,000 men in under two years — all but swamped the housing in Easter Ross. Every cottage, chalet, bungalow, bed-sit, boarding house, hotel and available house within miles of the Nigg yard was snapped up. And of course the desperate shortage had the effect of inflating the prices and rents to a very high level. "It's all right for the Americans," said one disgruntled Edinburgh man. "They get an overseas allowance. They can afford to pay up to thirty quid a week for a furnished house. We can't."

To be fair to Highland Fabricators, the company have at least tried to ameliorate the situation. Right at the outset they applied for planning permission to build labour camps at a number of sites on the Cromarty Firth. Each time the County Council turned them down flat. "The council felt that they didn't want a company town springing up," says John Robertson. "They wanted the men who worked at the yard to become part of the community, to belong to Easter Ross, family men housed in proper houses."

That was all very well, but the county had no way of building enough houses to cope with the demand from the Highland Fabricators employees. To put some kind of roofs over their employees' heads, Highland Fabricators brought in first one, then two elderly Greek cruise liners, known (not very affectionately) as the "Highland Queens". The ships have seen better days. Weighing 900 tons, and capable of housing up to 500 men, both were built on the Clyde and spent their lives plying the tourist routes of the Mediterranean. "Our lads," said the company newsletter, announcing the arrival of the first HQ, "should find the Highland Queen pretty hospitable, for apart from her comfortable cabins, she's equipped with a cinema, bar, library, TV and even swimming pool."

When they got aboard "our lads" were not so sure. Whatever it was, life aboard the Highland Queen was not luxury. A Stirlingshire welder, one of the first aboard the original HQ managed to secure himself one of the "good cabins". He lives in a minuscule, depressing little room with two bunks, a tiny dresser, a sink in one corner and very little else. The cabin is dimly lit, the paint-work is dismal and cracked, and the only decoration is the elderly lifeboat/lifejacket drill printed in Greek, French, Italian, Spanish, English and German.

"Claustrophobic," he describes it. "No other word. And living cooped up like this, you tend to get on one another's nerves. My mate, now, he works nights, and I work days. We're always waking one another up, that's a right piss-off, I can tell you. Or if we are on the same shift . . . well, maybe he drinks and you don't. So he comes in every night half pissed, and spews in the sink, so you get a bit narked. And before you know it . . ."

This accounts for the lurid stories of violence aboard the ships. All the men insist that the legends are either complete rubbish or wild exaggerations. But they do admit that, due to fatigue, boredom, drink, cards, and general irritation, fists occasionally fly. "Two kinds aboard the ships," observed an Edinburgh welder wryly. "Fellas with black eyes and fellas with sore hands."

Some of the men recall — with some fondness — the old days when visits from ladies were not unknown. "But that's all stopped now," a man explained. "We got to-

29

gether and sorted that out. All we do is watch the films, watch the telly, play cards or drink."

Accounts of the food vary according to tastes, but it is generally agreed to be pretty good. One Welsh travelling man was astounded at the sheer quality and size of the steaks. "Never seen anything like it man," he breathed. "My mate got three and took another one down to the site. Beautiful it was." Others are not so enthusiastic particularly about the Aegean cooking produced by the Greek crew. "Whit am I supposed to dae with a Moussaka," one Glaswegian grumbled.

Oddly perhaps, most of the men approve of the rather strict no-women/no-visitors rules. "For some blokes this ship is the only place they've got," a welder explains. "It's their only home. They keep everything they've got — record players, TV, radios, the lot, in their cabins. You can't have just *anybody* wandering about, can you? One lad broke his leg on the site, and lay in his bunk for six weeks. He just had nowhere else to go."

The company themselves are less than enchanted with the conditions aboard the Highland Queen, and very reluctant to have photographs taken aboard the ships. They concede that men living two or three to a small cabin is no substitute for a proper home and family but claim, that as things stand, there is very little they can do about the housing situation.

Another makeshift solution to the Easter Ross housing problem is, of course, the caravan. They have sprouted around most of the villages in Easter Ross, usually in ones or twos, but in greater numbers at Balintore, on the A9 near Dingwall, and down on the sand at Nigg point itself.

Balintore, for example, has thirty caravans. Officially the site is a summer-only site, and the caravans are supposed to move away in the autumn. But, the council explain, to move the people on would have caused unnecessary hardship, so they extended the licence for the duration of the housing crisis. Again, life in a caravan without mains electricity, with almost unspeakable toilet facilities, can be a pretty miserable business. "There is no electricity," said one young wife and mother, "so the only way to run a telly is off batteries. But that's too expensive for us. Only the single men — five or six of them to a van — can afford that."

A Leith man puts his point of view: "I'm pretty pissed off, I can tell you. I never see my wife except at occasional weekends and a fortnight in the summer. Last time I spoke to her on the phone she was really down in the dumps."

There are also a number of complaints (which are hard to bear out), that the local people are hostile to the caravan dwellers. "They treat us like tinkers sometimes," a woman says. "But we're not tinkers. We're decent hardworking folk. I've seen a woman just out of hospital cleaning out that toilet there with a hose. Just for her own satisfaction. Making sure its all right for her bairns. That's the kind of folk we are here."

Of all the clusters of caravans around Easter Ross, the dozen or so down among the dunes at Nigg Point are probably in the most difficult spot (from all points of view). They are on an unauthorised site, but they have been there for 2 years ,and if they can hang on for another year and a half this would be "permitted use", and then the council could not shift them.

And although Highland Fabricators disclaim responsibility for caravan housing, they have permission for a caravan site but have installed no hard standing, laid on no water, sewers, etc. Recently the Ross and Cromarty planning committee decided to put some pressure on the firm to provide a proper caravan site down at the point, and at least make life a bit more tolerable for some of their workers. "We are very worried about housing," say Highland Fabricators. "We are not attracting the kind of settled workforce we need. We're tending to get the travelling men." (In fact the company like to attribute their high rate of absenteeism — 20% a day — and turnover — 140% — to the lack of decent housing — although men in the yard are not so sure that that is the whole problem.) "A bachelor camp such as we have is a serious problem," Herb Nelson agrees. "We've got to have housing to have a stable work force."

When housing is discussed Highland Fabricators tend to strike a pious note, but the shortfall is as much their own fault as anyone's. In the course of building up the yard, the figures they gave to Ross and Cromarty County Council consistently underestimated the number of men they would employ. "I think quite frankly," said Lord Polwarth, once Minister of State in charge of oil development, and no enemy of the big companies, "when they originally approached the situation the companies might have co-operated a bit more closely with the local authorities in discussing their needs, before putting in the application."

For their part, the county council were inclined to be cautious. They had been bitten before, when the Grampian Chemicals scheme failed to come off, and when British Aluminium had overstated their requirement and the council were left with around fifty empty houses on their hands (long since occupied). And there was no guarantee (nor were Highland Fabricators prepared to give one) that the Nigg yard would last. Highland Fabricators, when pressed, will admit half-seriously, that there is not much at Nigg that could not be packed up and floated away. But Ross and Cromarty County Council had made some contingency plans. As far back as 1970 they saw the demand coming (or at least made a shrewd guess), and put forward an Amendment (No. 7) to their county development plan, to re-zone agricultural land around Alness for housing. There were objections (almost inevitable in a tightly-farmed area like Easter Ross), and a public inquiry was held early in 1971.

After hearing the pros and cons, the Reporter (Scottish version of the Inspector) then took 16 *months* to write his report, and the Scottish Office and Gordon Campbell (Conservative Secretary of State for Scotland) took a few months to consider it. In January 1973, almost two years after Ross and Cromarty had taken their initiative, Gordon Campbell decided that to re-zone the land for housing would be "premature".

"It was a fantastic decision," says John Robertson (who is one of the Scottish Office's most vociferous critics in the north). "They allow the primary effect to just rip, then mess about with the people who are trying to keep up with it. Personally, I think it's deliberate." (To be fair to St. Andrew's House, it should be said that in recent months the Scottish Special Housing Association has undertaken a 1,200 house three year programme, and as a temporary measure has bought a hundred or so houses from private contractors which are now let to tenants at a subsidised rent.)

The county council's latest attempt to sort out Easter Ross, plan its future and assign land for industry, agriculture, nature reserve, recreation, and of course housing was contained in Amendment No. 10 to the development plan. This amendment was, in principle, quite a piece of planning.

Twelve separate areas were earmarked for residential expansion: Tain and Lamington was seen virtually as a new town; Alness, Tor and Muir of Ord, and Dingwall were seen as medium sized towns; Conon Bridge, Evanton,

Invergordon designated as small towns; North Kessock, Seaboard Strathpeffer, Culbokie, Munlochy, Avoch, Fortrose and Cromarty were all to stay as villages. The total population which Easter Ross could support was put down as 160,000 — an enormous increase.

"Quite a lot hinges on Amendment No. 10," says George Pease, the county planning officer. "It would give us enough housing for a few years at least. Otherwise there will be enormous pressure for *ad hoc,* uncontrolled, and probably fairly squalid housing development."

In the event, Amendment No. 10 went through with a few minor changes. But the council's problems are far from over. Having earmarked the land they need to build on, they are now faced with the problems of finding materials and labour to build the houses. And almost every contractor in the area — including the council themselves — report a fairly desperate shortage of skilled labour.

"How can we build houses for the folk working at Nigg," complained one builder, "when all our men are down working at Nigg. We can't afford to pay them the kind of money they are getting there. And even if we had the men, we can hardly get the materials. When it's short like this, it all gets snapped up down south."

One way or another, putting one brick on top of another has become a fraught business in Easter Ross, complicated by labour shortages, material shortages, escalating prices, and transport costs. This does not bode well for the men languishing on the Highland Queens, in the caravans at Nigg point and Balintore, or paying £15-20 a week rent for two small rooms in a converted cottage next to nowhere.

5

In Easter Ross, housing is not the only amenity in short supply: everything is in short supply. There are not enough doctors, not enough nurses, clinics, baby clinics, not enough community centres, billiard halls, cinemas, school places, secondary school teachers, not enough of any of the components that a well run, healthy community needs.

"I estimate we need to spend at least £1 million a year for the next ten years just to improve our recreation facilities," says Roland Mardon, who has been converted from a pro-development enthusiast to one of the council's disenchanted. "We haven't even got enough buses to go round."

The men living on the ships and in caravans at Nigg are well aware of the shortage of places to go to and things to do. Their main form of recreation is drinking at the Nigg Ferry Hotel, sited neatly at the end of the gangway. The public bar, where most of the men drink is a big, chilly barn of a place, with a tiny coal fire at one end, a few chairs and tables, and a billiard table in the middle of the room.

The rumour is that the owner is the richest man in Easter Ross (Every man who has sunk a pint there knows "for a fact" that he has turned down £50,000/£75,000/£100,000/£500,000 for the Inn). Certainly a lot of drinking goes on. The work force tend to confine themselves to the public bar (where the beer, oddly, is sold in dimpled jars and not thin glasses), while the foremen and the middle management favour the lounge/cocktail bar.

Between the two bars a lot of ale and spirit is disposed. "But what else is there to do," a Glaswegian asks reasonably. "There is no bus service, at least none that you'd notice. A taxi to Tain costs you a couple of quid — if you can get one."

But for all the frontier-town air of the place, the big majority of the men who live on the ships and drink at the Nigg Ferry Hotel are hard working family men who want a steady job, a decent wage and a place for their family to live. Many of them are pretty sour about having to live a bachelor life in miserable conditions. There used to be a map on the wall of the Ferry Hotel. There was an arrow pointing to Nigg point. The legend read "You are here (hard luck Pal !)."

On a Friday night, one of the favourite destinations is the Balnagown Hotel in Tain which runs a (now famous) dance after the pubs shut. To the strains of tunes like "The Wild side of Life", as rendered by Caber Feidh (a local and very good Country and Western band), hundreds of Fife welders, Clydeside riggers, Dingwall bank clerks, London fabricators, Welsh travelling men, Texas gaffers, Louisiana weld-checkers, not to mention the Ross and Cromarty chapter of the Hells Angels, drink at the mobbed bar, and besiege the local bird life (By far the most successful in that respect, with their natty white sweaters and white bell-bottoms are the Greek crewmen from the Highland Queens).

The Balnagown dances have quite a reputation in Tain ("a douce wee place" according to John Robertson). There are dark hints among the citizens of dreadful goings on. But in fact they are highly enoyable. The band is always good, the dancing is high-spirited (to say the least), the drinks are cheap, the company is out to enjoy itself, and the local ladies have the time of their lives being outnumbered and heavily pursued by a cosmopolitan crowd.

Predictably, every now and again, fists and bottles fly, but the bouncers are fast and methodical. And according to one of the ladies at the bar, "It's our own lads that are the worst for starting trouble. Especially the boys from Caithness and Stornoway. The Greek boys, now, they are awfully quiet. No trouble at all."

Come Sunday, much the same clientele moves ten miles west to the village of Portmahomack, where the Caledonian Hotel has extended itself to lay on a large, spacious and well-equipped dance floor, bar and lounge. The "Caley" dances tend to be slightly better dressed affairs, with perhaps a higher proportion of locals. The drinks are more expensive. The atmosphere is more suburban lounge bar, and the band favours noisy, reasonably accurate rock and roll.

Basically amiable and good natured though it is, all in all the local police have problems. "Quite a work load we have now," the spokesman for Ross & Sutherland police says. "More people, more money, and more of it being spent on drink." Nothing serious, the police insist, just outbreaks of small-scale violence. And nothing like as bad as the days when they were building the hydro dams back in the hills.

"They used to tell us that when the "oil men" came, our women wouldn't be able to walk the streets without being ravaged," one policeman recalls with amusement. "Well if they are being ravaged they must be enjoying it, because they're not telling us about it . . ."

But while they appreciate the absence of the anticipated wave of serious crime, the local police are worried. "Our resources are very stretched," they say. "We have a real shortage of constables. We are losing men every month. Most are going to Nigg either to work on the site, or as security guards. Our total force is 160 men, so if we lose, say eight men, that's 5% of the force. And young men

37

are not becoming constables. They can get much better money elsewhere. Occasionally, we get a local officer who has become tired of life in the south, or with the Metropolitan Police. But they are pretty few and far between. It's a serious problem and we think it will get worse." The police point out that while there has been no huge increase in crime, that is only part of their problem. Increased traffic means more accidents, incidents and snarl-ups on the roads to sort out. The influx of foreign-born workers means more work for the Home Office, checking work permits, immigration regulations etc. The increase in the number of families means more lost children, absconding teenagers, husband/wife aggravation and so on.

Much the same kind of load is being put on the county's welfare services. There are now not enough probation officers, welfare officers, or district nurses. The area council of social service has been among the most consistent and sharpest critics of the speed of industrial development.

The education authorities are keeping a sharp eye on the situation, without sounding any alarm. "Our main concern is the sporadic nature of the development," says one of the education authority spokesmen. "We tend to make our arrangements from the housing programme — 0.6 children per new house, 0.45 primary children per new house — that kind of projection. Now at the moment, with this housing shortage, we are not too sure where we are. We could be surprised if more people come up the A9 in caravans. But then again, the Highland Queen situation — hundreds of men without their families — is no problem to us."

Primary schools, it seems, are no problem. "A lot of these village schools were built to accommodate far more kids than are using them now. If the numbers build up, there will be plenty of space there. Teachers are another matter, of course, but this area has always been a teacher-producing area."

Nor has the intake of children from other parts of the country (and other parts of the world) posed any great problem. "Most of the kids come from other parts of Scotland," the education authority say, "so their standards are pretty much the same as ours. And the American kids — well, they tend to be from management-class families: pretty bright, and highly motivated. They slot in quite well. Most of them seem to go to Tain Royal Academy."

The county education committee clearly feel they can cope, so long as they are informed of the house-building rate, and, "Our only concern is caravans," they say. "You can haul them up the A9 tomorrow and have instant housing. We could be surprised that way. And we would find a sudden school-building programme difficult to cope with. There's a shortage of building materials and a shortage of labour, furniture, equipment and books are not too easy to come by either."

6

Inevitably, big oil trails with it big money. Exploiting an oilfield, especially a submarine field, is a complex, difficult and very expensive business. There are drilling rigs to be built and serviced, huge production platforms to be designed and assembled with their elaborate and costly entrails, there are submarine pipe-lines to be coated and laid from big barges, there are tank farms and tanker terminals to be constructed, and there is always the prospect of refineries, gas processing plant or petro-chemical works. It adds up to a multi-million pound complex of industries.

And the areas on which these industries descend — areas such as the Cromarty Firth — become prime sites which attract the attention of the development companies. Some are big, well-run, well-banked and responsible organisations; others are small, under-financed, and not so reputable. Of all the speculative developers attracted by the oil generated action on the Cromarty Firth, the biggest, most powerful, most ambitious, and most con-troversial was the Cromarty Firth Development Company.

The Cromarty Firth Development Company is one of the four operating arms of an Edinburgh registered firm of developers called Onshore Investments Ltd. (note the initials OIL). And Onshore Investments Ltd is the wholly-owned subsidiary of a Lancashire property firm called Mount St. Bernard Trust, which, in turn, is owned by a firm called Blue Oak Ltd. The brain presiding over this clutch of companies (plus a number of others) is a north of England business man called John Foulerton, from Grange over Sands in Lincolnshire.

Mount St. Bernard Trust was set up by Foulerton, John Wolff, and John Wollam and Michael Higgin (rep-resentatives of the up and coming merchant bank Edward Bates). In 1972, half of the Mount St. Bernard shares were bought by the Edinburgh-run fund Atlantic Assets and the board was then joined by Stewart Newton and Ian Rushbrook of Ivory & Sime, the Edinburgh fund managers.

In the same year, Onshore Investments was registered in Edinburgh, operating from a solicitors' office in Hope Street, with a nominal capital of £1 million. The directors were Foulerton, his associates John Wolff, and Ian Peters of Hythe in Cheshire, plus an Edinburgh solicitor Charles

Fraser, who was a director of North Sea Assets Property, Atlantic Assets, British Assets, second British Assets, and Edward Bates.

Onshore then decided to operate in the likely areas of Scotland through four separate companies. Business in Shetland was to be looked after by a firm called "Nordport" (lifting the name from Zetland County Council's own project), having hired the services of a local and trusted businessman called Ian Caldwell. Around Aberdeen and the north-east, development was to take place through Peterhead and Fraserburgh Estates (directors, Ian Peters, Charles Fraser and a local solicitor called John Smith). There was also an interesting 50-50 tie-up with another developer called Site Preparations of Glasgow, through the Buchan Development Company.

But the biggest of the four companies (and, as it turned out, the biggest spender) was the Cromarty Firth Development Company. This operation was set up in June 1972 under the name of Scottish Technopark Estates (the name was changed in October that year). In charge was Ian Peters, managing director of Onshore Investments, ex-Royal Engineer, and a qualified quantity surveyor and cost consultant. Representing the Edinburgh money was Charles Fraser, and the other director was Donald Firth, once a trainee foreign exchange dealer with a London Bank, and now marketing administrator with Onshore Investments.

Cromarty Firth Development were fast off the mark. In July 1972 they bought 376 acres of flat coastal land at Delny, near Invergordon, from Grampian Chemicals for £490,496. At the same time they bought 220 acres at Nigg Point (which Grampian Chemicals had bought from John Robertson) for another £480,490. In two deals they had bought two of the best industrially-zoned sites on the Cromarty Firth.

At the end of the year Cromarty Firth Development were joined by Dr Ian Skewis, a former executive of the Highlands and Islands Development Board, and, early in 1973, by the distinguished and influential Sir James Mackay, formerly Deputty Chairman of the H&IDB. (The departure of public officials to private enterprise did not go unnoticed in parliament.)

Meanwhile the buying went on. In December Cromarty Firth started to buy land in and around Fearn airfield: a local farmer, George Budge, was paid £423,000 for his 280 acres around the airfield. David Sutherland, of Tullich Farm, was paid £402,000 for 178 acres near the village of Balintore. At Nigg, the seventeen acres which Hunter Gordon had sold to Petroleum Land Holdings were bought by Cromarty Firth for more than £28,000. A stretch of foreshore at Nigg point, which had changed hands in 1961 for £4,000 was bought by Cromarty Firth from one Dennis Tipping for £40,000. Pollo Farm, between the Cromarty Firth and the Delny site, was sold to the company, and they paid over £1 million for the rest of Hunter Gordon's farm Pitcalzean Mains. They also entered a long, protracted (and in the end fruitless) negotiation to buy the big coastal site of Balintraid farm from the Forsyth family.

It was quite a spending spree. In a year and a half the Cromarty Firth Development Company had spent more than £3 million. But at the end of it the company held more than 3,500 acres of the best land in and around Easter Ross, and by March 1973, they were promising great things.

The stretches of land at Delny and Pollo were to be ". . . developed as a huge 600 acre industrial estate known as Cromarty Firth MIDAS . . .", from which the company visualised ". . . a pier giving access to the deepwater together with the construction of docks . . ." (yet another

42

deepwater harbour project for the Cromarty Firth). The land at Nigg, already zoned for oil storage and tanker terminal, was seen as incorporating ". . . a wider range of activities based on and including oil refining." Nor was that all. The old airfield at Fearn was to be re-opened ". . . for full scale commercial flying; the Company plan to change its name to Cromarty Firth Airport and hope to arrange scheduled services linking Inverness with Inverness Airport . . ." Another, small-scale industrial site was to be developed on the land around the airport.

There was to be housing too. A deal was made with a local builder Hugh Macrae to form a joint company to build the houses needed for the ". . . controlled and planned inward manpower flow programme". Not just posh houses either, but houses ". . . aimed at the working man, catering for persons who might normally be expected to be council house tenants."

But the best laid plans etc. If anything, the manoeuverings of Cromarty Firth Development Company were too successful, the machine too well oiled. Coupled with the very similar operations taking place in the Shetlands, and the land buying around Peterhead, the whole Onshore Investments project backfired in the middle of 1973.

Much of the money invested in Onshore Investments and the Mount St. Bernard Trust was Edinburgh money. Two highly respectable (and respected) Edinburgh investments funds held big stakes in Foulerton's operations; Atlantic Assets owned 50% of Mount St. Bernard and North Sea Assets had options to buy 50% of Onshore Investments. Both Edinburgh funds were managed by Ivory & Sime.

But the speed, and in some cases tactlessness, with which the Onshore companies worked, stirred up a hornets' nest of Scottish Labour M.P.s and accusations began to fly about the "Edinburgh Mafia of financial in-

stitutions", selling Scotland out from under its people. The
Edinburgh money men were, reputedly, deeply shocked
by the charges, with the result that both investment funds
backed sharply out of both Mount St. Bernard and Onshore Investments, although North Sea Assets kept their
options partly opened. (This name-calling and mud-slinging
was one of the main reasons that Dr Ian Skewis, and later
Sir James Mackay, resigned from the company at the
beginning of 1973.)

It was a blow which left Onshore Investments gasping,
and badly under-financed. Six months later Ian Peters
was attempting to put a brave face on the setback by
saying that "we genuinely felt we would benefit from
industrial, rather than financial investment. We're basically
an industrial development company, you see." He was
also at some pains to berate the delays and upsets involved in getting anything done. "It is absolutely essential
for activities to move as rapidly as they possibly can,"
Peters said. "Any delay is absolutely catastrophic."

Some observers were quick to note that the Cromarty
Firth Development Company might have done themselves
a disservice. Late in 1973 John Robertson said: "I think
Cromarty Firth may have put themselves in something
of a box. They have spent nearly £4 million in this area.
Somehow they must begin to get that money back, and
fairly soon."

But that, as Robertson pointed out, will clash with the
council's plans. "The council wants to build up steadily,"
he explains," at a rate approaching 500 to 600 jobs per
annum. We don't want a massive surge, then a falling
off. I think there will be problems with Cromarty Firth
when they start promoting their plans . . ."

But that was reckoning without the spiralling increase
in the interest rates. Cromarty Firth, and the other
Onshore Investments Companies, were suddenly faced

44

with enormous service charges running on the money they had borrowed to finance their land deals. And at the same time the industrial backers they were looking for proved very elusive, and Cromarty County Council less than pliable.

By the end of the year the Cromarty Firth Development Company were running out of time (and possibly money). In August 1973, instead of becoming involved in the refinery project at Nigg, they simply sold all their land there to an American company. At the beginning of 1974 they applied for permission to build houses on 174 acres of land they owned at Bayfield near Fearn-airfield. The application was turned down.

By the end of 1973, all properties and assets of all the Nordport companies, both present and future, had been signed over by bond and floating charge to the London merchant bankers, William Brandt and Son. Clearly the Onshore Investments companies were having to pull their horns in very sharply. In late June, Brandt's were saying that while the companies were "still in an operating and trading situation", nevertheless, "their development activities have been curtailed."

The bankers also said firmly that strict financial control was being exercised over the companies' spending, and that letters had been sent out stopping all credit to the four companies. All existing credit had been referred to the Unicentre in Preston, home of John Foulerton's clutch of companies.

All was not well with Onshore Investments. Their elegant offices in Rutland Street in the West End of Edinburgh are mostly closed, and no-one is answering the telephone. When pressed, Ian Peters explained the problems of the companies. "We are having to rationalise the organisation," he admits. "In the end it didn't seem to make much sense having four separate boards, one for each company. We are now concentrating all our activities in one board in London." He denied that the office was closed, said they were having some trouble with the telephones, and said that it would be best to contact him at his home telephone number. Peters assigns his troubles to the "staggering rate of interest being charged on money" and the general industrial climate. "It's not healthy. No one wants to crash and *do* anything. Everyone is waiting around to see what is going to happen."

More recently, there are indications that Onshore Investments have found backing, and are thinking of starting a petrochemical plant at Peterhead.

Onshore Investments Ltd. were not, perhaps, the most popular of the companies who moved into the Cromarty Firth. But there are a lot of people who will be sorry to see them cut back, or even cancel their operations. The Delny site where they planned their MIDAS estate has been zoned for industry for years, and is one of the best industrial sites in Scotland. If industrialism is going to happen on the Cromarty Firth (and it is hard to see it being halted) Delny/Pollo is where it should happen. It also made sense to try and do something with the Fearn airfield. The road connection to Inverness is dismal and lengthy and the air network could stand a stop between Inverness and Wick.

But, in the summer of 1974, after years of big-scale talk, Delny and Pollo are still farmland. The land around Bayfield earmarked for housing has not been built on, and Fearn airfield is as derelict and unused as ever, except by Sunday-morning model aeroplane buffs.

7

On 12 June 1973 a new company called Alphaclass Investment Developments was set up at the office of McRobert and Son, Solicitors, of 91 West George Street, Glasgow. At the end of August of that year Alphaclass Investment Developments bought 236 acres of land around Nigg point from the Cromarty Firth Development Company. The land, for which they paid £840,388, was an industrially-zoned stretch which had changed hands three times in the course of a few years.

In October 1973 Alphaclass changed their name, and adopted the very Scottish sounding title of the Cromarty Petroleum Company. But the file they have lodged in Companies House in Edinburgh contains a list of American names, American addresses and details of American resources. Cromarty Petroleum, as was later announced, was a subsidiary of Universe Tankships Inc., which is the shipping arm of the giant American group, National Bulk Carriers.

National Bulk Carriers are a powerful organisation, one of the biggest privately-owned companies in the world, owned and run by Daniel Ludwig of New York. They are primarily a shipping group, with a fleet of huge ships carrying iron ore, bauxite, coal and, of course, crude oil. They were one of the first shipping firms to realise the potential of huge cargoes carried in vast ships, and have for years been building up a fleet of VLCCs (Very Large Crude Carriers), mainly oil tankers. They have six ships of 326,000 tons which run from the Persian Gulf to Bantry Bay in the west of Ireland.

Like almost every large group, National Bulk Carriers have diversified. They mine coal in Australia and the U.S.A., and iron ore, bauxite and kaolin in Brazil. They grow oranges in Panama, rice and timber in Brazil, and ranch cattle in Venezuela. They also build houses in the United States, Central America, Indonesia, Mexico, Australia and South Africa. Overall their assets run into billions of dollars, and they employ more than 20,000 people in twenty countries.

Over the past few years, National Bulk Carriers have been expanding their oil related activities. They joined a drilling consortium to explore the Irish Sea, and were involved with Gulf Oil running a refinery in Panama. Refineries make eminent sense to NBC: why run crude oil to other people's refineries when you can take it to your own? So on 12 December 1973 NBC's subsidiary, the Cromarty Petroleum Company, asked the Ross and Cromarty County Council for permission to build an oil refinery storage tanks and a tanker terminal at Nigg point.

The Cromarty project included £150 million worth of buildings, equipment, instrumentation, storage tanks, pipeline and tanker terminal, designed to suck in crude from the North Sea and elsewhere, crack it, and reduce it to naphtha, benzine, kerosene and, of course, petroleum. The refinery itself was to be built on the rough, gently sloping land in the lee of the Hill of Nigg. More than 420 million gallons of oil were to be stored in vast storage caverns 100 feet under the sand dunes at Nigg point, with another 735 million gallons stored in huge tanks. A tanker loading jetty, capable of handling NBC's vast 450,000 ton tankers, was to project a thousand feet out into the Firth between the Sutors of Cromarty. The whole scheme would swallow up 570 acres of land, and require two thousand men to build it. Once in operation the project would provide work for 350 skilled men.

The scheme exploded like a depth charge in the already troubled waters of Easter Ross. This was the real thing, industry with a vengeance. For years, ever since the mid-1960s, the area had been alive with rumours, speculation, gossip and hope about the prospect of the petrochemical industry arriving in strength, but this was the first tangible scheme.

"The refinery was *exactly* the kind of project we had been looking for," says John Robertson, who has been an enthusiastic supporter of almost all developments around the Cromarty Firth. "You could say that the logic of all we had been hoping for converged on the refinery project."

But not everyone in Easter Ross was as enthusiastic as John Robertson. Among many who were as firmly opposed to the project as he was in favour was Roland Mardon, a local farmer, councillor and member of the planning committee. "We have nearly 2,000 people on our housing list," he says, "and we're only building 1,300 houses. It will be years before we can house everyone who needs it. We have no social amenities. We need to spend about £1 million a year for ten years on amenities — cinemas, skiing, skating, community centres. There are already 3,500 jobs in the pipeline. We must give ourselves a breathing space of four to five years just to catch up."

The council officers were inclined to be cautious. For three years they had been run ragged trying to cope with shortages of every sort of amenity — schools, clinics, community centres, transport and, above all, housing. They wanted to take a good hard look at the Cromarty Petroleum Scheme. "So we commissioned three separate schemes," says Mr Brindley, deputy planning officer, "one to look at pollution and safety measures, that kind of thing, one to look at the amount of noise generated and another, a firm of landscape architects, to assess the visual aspect. We also asked the new Port Authority to take a look at the problem of big tankers in the Firth, and our own planning department for an impact study." The council also decided to ask St. Andrew's House whether Scotland really needed a refinery.

While the various council-appointed experts were busy testing, drilling, sampling, measuring and assessing, Cromarty Petroleum were busy fixing. For one thing, they did not have all the land they needed — far from it. They only owned 236 acres, and they badly needed the stretch of land north of Nigg point. This was the land that Robert Hunter Gordon had agreed to sell to the Cromarty Firth Development Company. After weeks of discussion with the now troubled developers the negotiators from Cromarty Petroleum bought the 621 acres of Pitcalzean Mains farm for about £1 million. The deal was finalised on 26 March 1974 and gave Cromarty Petroleum more than 850 acres of mixed farmland and a stretch of seashore.

As soon as they had lodged their application, Cromarty Petroleum began a campaign to convince the citizens of Easter Ross that the refinery project was a good idea. They organised two meetings, one at Nigg and one on the other side of the Firth in the little town of Cromarty (whose town council had been among the objectors). Cromarty's town hall was crowded the night that the men from Pittsburgh and New York came to put their case.

"The reaction was very mixed," says one of the audience, "but the split was classic. The white settlers and the middle class were out in force, agitating about the countryside being despoiled and the air being polluted, and so on. The local people were cautious, but inclined to approve. At least that's the way I see it." Duncan

McPherson, who is the county councillor for Cromarty, agrees that reaction was hard to gauge: "the people did want the jobs; but I think they were sceptical about the company."

For more than four years the people of Easter Ross had been taking sides on the issue of whether or not to allow industrial development. Once again early in 1974, the battle lines began to form. In favour of the refinery were most of the small businessmen and shopkeepers, the trade unions, the local Labour Party, the Liberals (John Robertson is their candidate), the S.N.P., and Hamish Gray the Conservative M.P. Opposed to the refinery were most of the big farmers, the landowning gentry and aristocracy, the retired people from the south, local business based on tourism, conservationists, nauralists and, of course, the people living in the immediate vicinity.

In Tain, Evanton, Dingwall, Alness, Portmahomack, Balintore, and Cromarty the refinery became the hot topic. The ins and outs were wrangled over in every pub, club, village hall, board room and council chamber in Easter Ross. The local press was full of the subject, correspondence and petitions began to circulate. By the time all the objections were added up, there were 197 in all, seventy from letters and the rest from petitions.

The Cromarty Petroleum Company joined in the great debate by circulating a "newsletter" to "keep you informed of developments concerning our proposed oil refinery." Issue number One, dated 26 April 1974, was a straightforward information sheet concerning the Pitcalzean Mains deal, the number of objections, the company telephone number, the information that Dunskeath Castle down at Nigg point was to be preserved, together with some useful details about National Bulk Carriers and the managing director of Cromarty

51

Petroleum, E. D. Loughney, and his ". . . fifty years' experience in the mainstream of the oil industry". Newsletter number Two, however, was an altogether subtler document. It appeared on 14 June, just two weeks before the crucial debates on the refinery. As well as including some technical details of the storage caverns, the tanker terminal and the prowess of the company's consultants, it went to great lengths to stress the fact that the company had been working hand in glove with the various authorities — with the County Council over housing, with the Port Authority over shipping, and with the government inspectorates over safety and pollution.

The newsletter also struck an interesting (and possibly dangerous) political note. In the course of their argument in favour of the refinery scheme, heavy emphasis was laid on the Scottish economy and Scottish industry. "We have also noted a report," says the newsletter, referring to a highly speculative piece in the *Scotsman*, "which says that there is a plan 'under active consideration,' for a trunk pipeline to transport the bulk of oil from Scottish waters, direct to England . . ." Cromarty Petroleum go on to explain how this indicates ". . . the extent to which existing refinery distribution influences much current thinking about North Sea oil." The politically loaded implication is that if Scotland wants to keep the oil she had better have some refineries of her own.

Four days before the Planning and Development Committee were due to make their decision, committee members received the reports of their various consultants. According to Torquil Nicolson, convenor of the planning committee, "the technical report from Cremer . . . said the atmospheric and water pollution would be well within acceptable limits. The plan was very good, in fact. There was some concern about spillage from tankers, but that was all. The acoustic consultants said the noise level

52

would be acceptable. But the landscape architects recommended refusal. They said the whole thing should be rearranged." The council's own impact study said that it would be a struggle but they thought they could just about cope.

Everyone on the committee, whether for or against, and including the impartial county clerk, was sharply critical of the amount of time taken by the Scottish Development Department to answer the request for information about the economic need for refineries. "We wrote fifteen letters, had four meetings and made ten 'phone calls," says John Robertson, "and finally we got a letter which was complete mumbo-jumbo — no use at all." (In defence of St. Andrew's House it could be pointed out that the request had to go from Edinburgh to the Department of Energy in London, and back.)

On the afternoon of Monday 24 June 1974, the Ross and Cromarty Planning and Development Committee debated the Nigg point refinery project. For more than three hours the discussion went on, while E. D. Loughney and his colleagues sweated it out in the corridor outside, answering questions when called. Eventually the vote was taken, John Robertson proposing the motion, Roland Mardon opposing. There were seven votes in favour and eight against; Torquil Nicolson, the convenor, abstained. The farmers and gentry of the landward areas and the west had carried the day: the Earl of Cromartie from Strathpeffer, Mrs Caie of Loch Broom, Lt-Commander Dumas of Gairloch, Roland Mardon of Rosskeen West, Captain Richardson of Kincardine, Roderick Stirling of Urray and Douglas McPherson of Cromarty. The result might have been different if Provost MacRae of Dingwall and Mrs Rhind of Pollo House had been able to attend the meeting ("We would definitely have voted in favour," says Provost MacRae.)

Roland Mardon explained why he moved rejection: "For one thing we didn't have enough time to study the consultants' reports. Then there was the council's impact study, and the information coming from the Port Authority. And also I did not think the company gave us enough information on which to make up our minds." But no matter what the reports might have said, Mardon's main objection, which was shared by others, is that the area is overloaded with industry and incomers, and there are just not enough houses, schools, hospitals, clinics, doctors, community centres and roads to cope: "we need at least four years, maybe longer, to catch up with the problems we have now."

Duncan MacPherson of Cromarty explains his objections to the scheme: "This company have not sufficient experience in refining. I'd need a lot more information before I could be happy. If a refinery had been in the national interest I would have supported it. But the SDD letter was very inconclusive." McPherson also doubts the large-scale economics of the project: "it's an American firm, American finance, and all the profits would go to America. If we must have a refinery, why not a BP refinery?"

But their arguments did nothing to assuage the disappointment, and in some cases anger, of the refinery enthusiasts. "I think we'll be the laughing stock of the country," said Provost Ferguson of Tain; "a ludicrous decision" (John Robertson); "very disappointing" (Provost MacRae of Dingwall); "I always regarded Ross and Cromarty as a progressive authority," (Rev, Murdo Nicolson of Urray, bitterly) "but this decision will be interpreted as the policy of a council which is timid and afraid, with no desire to see progress or revitalisation in Scotland."

To the extreme gratification of the Cromarty Petroleum

Company their supporters leapt into action. Almost every councillor was deluged by telephone calls and letters of complaint. The shop stewards at the Highland Fabricators' yard, who like the idea of long-term employment in the area, whipped up a petition with 2,000 signatures within days. "the reaction has been incredible," says John Robertson. "I've had 120 'phone calls all saying 'My God, we must have this refinery'. No opposition 'phone calls: 120 to nil." (Roland Mardon, of course, claims that all his calls have expressed the opposite sentiment.)

There seems little doubt that there was a genuine up-surge of resentment against the decision of the planning committee, so much so that the full council decided on 27 June to ask the convenor of the committee to reconsider. The convenor, Torquil Nicolson, agreed to take the matter back even if it meant suspending standing orders to do so.

The Cromarty Petroleum Company made it clear that while they were "disappointed" at losing the first round, and would be even more disappointed to lose the second, they would fight on. They made it clear that if the vote went against them again they would appeal to the Secretary of State for Scotland. Government policy in the summer of 1974 made it unlikely that the Secretary of State would hesitate to overrule the Council.

On 30 July 1974 the planning committee met to reconsider their decision, and, as expected, they reversed their decision. The vote in favour of the refinery development was twelve to five.

8

How much more industry can Easter Ross take? The calculation is hard to make, and to a large extent depends on what is regarded as the optimum level of industrialisation. There are already plenty of people in the area (and outside it) crying stop ! enough ! There is a strong element of reaction and conservatism among the objectors, but their motives are not without honour. Landowners, farmers and the agricultural industry are genuinely troubled by the drift of men away from agriculture and forestry into higher-paid industries. They argue that at a time of growing shortages of food and timber this is a movement the country can ill afford. They also contend that too much valuable high-grade farmland is being zoned and then swallowed up by industry.

But the arguments in favour of development are more powerful. "Of course we've got problems," says one Easter Ross observer, "but at least they're the problems of life. And that makes a change, believe me. It's all very well worrying about the effects on the simple life, the effects on the grass and the dunes on Nigg Bay, the effects on the ducks and all the rest of it. But for generations we've watched our youngsters pack up and drift south looking for work; and the fact that education around here has always been pretty good just aggravated it. Just what is there for an educated youngster to *do* in Easter Ross? Well, now it's beginning, just beginning to go into reverse. And if we can build up a proper industrial base, if we can get some industrial *depth* into the area, then the services, the technology, the electronics

and all the rest will follow. And that means jobs: more important it means careers, some kind of fulfilment in the north. It may even mean colleges and teacher training schools. Let the London newspapers, the gentry and the southerners bleat all they like. North Sea oil represents a way out of generations of neglect, decay, demoralisation and exploitation. If I'm going to be exploited, I'd rather be exploited for a half-decent wage than work on some bugger's estate."

There are many in Easter Ross and the counties round about, especially among the working class, who feel this way. And every time the issue of development is put to the test in a local election, the pro-development platform wins, usually overwhelmingly. There is no doubt that most people north of Inverness approve whole-heartedly of North Sea oil and everything it has brought to Easter Ross — which, given the history of the northern Highlands, is hardly surprising. The eastern part of Ross (and of Sutherland) suffered most cruelly from the clearances. Almost every strath and glen from Beauly up to Caithness was ruthlessly cleared to make way for sheep and stag. The people were forced down to the coast to eke out a meagre existence fishing or, more usually, were forced to take passage for somewhere else. The actions of the local gentry in the nineteenth century were so heavy-handed and callous that Easter Ross was the scene of several small-scale rebellions, which were brutally put down by the constabulary and the army. The virtual obliteration of smallholdings and the building up of flocks of sheep and sporting estates systematically reduced the options of the local people. They are (or were until recently) confined to fishing, running small businesses, working for the forestry commission or the local council or, more likely, working on the farms and estates of the big landowners.

The appearance of industrial development on the horizon looked like the sun rising over Easter Ross. There was great excitement in the 1960s over the Grampian Chemicals proposals for a petrochemical complex. The scheme came to nothing, but it generated a lot of hopes at the time, and the awareness that Easter Ross, or at least the land around the Cromarty Firth, could be developed. Then came the smelter, which had the support of the council and the people. And finally the oil industry arrived.

But no community is ever unanimous about anything, and the coming of the oil developers raised many doubts and objections. Among the first to suffer were the people who live in the immediate vicinity of the developments, particularly the large Highland Fabricators' yard. Most of these live in the dozen or so small cottages which stretch up the road from Nigg point up to Ankerville. For several years they have had to put up with the noise, dust and vibrations, the road widening schemes, the sight of heavy lorries and the clamour from the yard itself. It would be senseless to deny that their lives have been disrupted and possibly ruined. The fact that most of them are elderly is especially unfortunate. Brown and Root could have done themselves some good by offering these people suitable accommodation elsewhere. It would not have cost them much, but it would have kept a number of people happy and would have improved the company's image locally. It could also be argued that the Council should have assumed some kind of special responsibility to protect the people from the impact of the yard. The truth is that small numbers of people are involved, and only those in the immediate vicinity. Nearby farms, like John Robertson's Castlecraig, are entirely out of sight and earshot of the yard, though not more than a mile away.

The environmental argument has been well aired over the past few years. It is true that Nigg Bay is an area of some natural interest, and that it gives shelter and sustenance to a number of species of duck and wildfowl. It is an interesting area, but nothing special, and disruption is unlikely to have a serious or permanent effect on the birdlife of Scotland. Naturalists admit that the building of the yard at Nigg point has had very little effect indeed.

The other plank of the environmental argument is the visual intrusion of the yard. It is enormous, and so are the structures it is designed to hold. The spectacular beauty of the Sutors of Cromarty will not be improved by the arrival of the oilfield platforms. But of all the areas of northern Scotland, Easter Ross is perhaps the least renowned for its scenery. The geography of the area as a whole is unspectacular, pleasant in a low-key way, with some interesting hill country not far away. It in no way compares with the stunning topography of the west coast, the straths of Sutherland or the high sea cliffs of Caithness.

It may be that, of all the areas of northern Scotland which could be industrialised, Easter Ross is the most suitable. Besides, the area has been gradually industrialised for some years, with small industrial estates, the Navy facility and storage tanks at Invergordon, the distilleries and now the aluminium smelter.

It has also been pointed out that anyone could drive through Easter Ross without catching sight of the Highland Fabricators' yard (if they didn't look too closely). Nigg point is well off the beaten tourist track, and is only visible from a few points on the A9, though from the town of Cromarty on the opposite Sutor it is all too visible.

Another objection, which is partially valid, is that

the industrial developments are eating into valuable and much-needed farmland. The Highland Fabricators' yard occupies 150 acres, but most of that was reclaimed fore-shore or reconstituted sand and duneland. The aluminium smelter swallowed up far more land, and the land occupied by MK-Shand was, in fact, leased from British Aluminium. So far the total loss has been quite small.

It might be a different story if the various development plans were to go ahead. The six hundred acres at Delny and Pollo which have been scheduled for industrial use are of very high quality (scale 2 and 3 on the five-point Macaulay Institute soil classification). Similarly the ramifications of the Nigg point refinery will consume a lot of excellent farmland. National Bulk Carriers are talking about continuing to farm as much as possible, but for economic return industry has far more to offer than agriculture.

Some hoteliers claim that thanks to the spread of industrialisation, the well-heeled southern tourists will drive straight through Easter Ross to more picturesque pastures without spending any money in the area. But others are disenchanted with tourism, which they see as a plague and a disease, resulting in a mentality of dependence. The tourist trade is highly seasonal, providing badly-paid jobs in the summer and few or none in the winter. The inadequate roads are jammed with chains of caravans, trailers and tent-laden motor cars. The countryside comes out in a rash of hot-dog stands, caravan sites, trinket shops and Granny's Hieland Hame Teashops. "And it's turning the north into a fucking zoo," says one irate Sutherland man. "What are we supposed to do? Stand about looking picturesque, being gawped at by tourists. Because that's what tourism does. I know a man who, in the summer, gets all dressed up in a kilt, plaid, feathered bonnet, takes his bagpipes, and goes and stands in Glengarry; and charges the tourists for taking pictures of him. Is that what they want for us, these folk who talk about the bad effect the oil will have on the tourists?"

There is also the more subtly-held objection that the kind of industry which the oilfields bring will disrupt and change for ever the way of life enjoyed by the people of Easter Ross. It is not an objection which gets much support from the people whose way of life is about to be disrupted. They see it as patronising and insulting, a point of view held mainly by retired people and in-comers from the south, those who moved north in order to remove themselves from urban living.

"What's so special about our way of life anyway?" asks one local man sourly. "We get up, go to our work, come home, watch the telly. The amount of money most of us get we can't afford to swan about buying holiday cottages, fishing in somebody's salmon river, skiing in the winter, all that stuff we're supposed to enjoy. A lot of us can't afford a car to enjoy all that scenery we're supposed to have at our doorstep."

In many ways the eastern Highlands, especially around Easter Ross, are indistinguishable from central Scotland. Not many people speak Gaelic, for example: there are far fewer Gaelic speakers in Easter Ross than there are in Glasgow. The Kirk does not have the hold on the imagination and life of the people that it does in parts of the north-west Highlands. There is nothing particularly distinctive about the way of life in Easter Ross — no more than in any other pleasant rural area of Scotland.

Some sardonic observers suggest that the local establish-ment are agitated by the political changes that are likely to occur following the arrival of the oil industry. Ross and Cromarty is the only constituency north of (and including) Inverness which has a Conservative M.P. A large influx of labour from the south, especially from Clydeside, is likely to make some impression on the Conservative majority. And wherever a part of Scotland has been galvanised by oil, the Scottish National Party have moved in fast. They are making heavy gains in the Ross and Cromarty area, coming second in the General Election of February 1974, and with a good chance of winning the seat next time round.

Of all the objections to the developments, the one which has most substance is that the local authorities, the community and the economy just cannot cope with the scale and the speed of industrialisation. One critical problem is housing, but this could be solved. It must be said in favour of the authorities that after years of delay and procrastination, they are now being allowed to take more decisive action to cope. The SSHA, for instance, has a considerable programme in hand for Easter Ross. They have been buying private housing from contractors to let, at subsidised rents, to workers. They have also been looking closely at the various timber systems used in Scandinavia. The recently approved Amendment No. 10 to the County Development Plan has rezoned most of the land that the county needs for housing over the next few years. In the long term there are plans to build a substantial new town in the area south of Tain, and to reinforce some of the villages (like Balintore). Another hopeful sign is that from 1975 the problems will be shared with the new Highland Region authority, a much bigger, better-equipped and better-financed organisation.

Easter Ross has its problems, but they are the "problems of life", unquestionably, and they are problems which can be solved with goodwill, expertise, planning and money. Compared with the scale of development taking place elsewhere in Britain, developments which have shakier *raisons d'etre*, the events in Easter Ross are insignificant. They do not compare in size with, for example, the Milton Keynes new town, designed for a population of nearly 250,000, or the now-suspended Maplin port/airport complex, or even an urban motorway scheme.

There is no way of preventing the oil industry moving into Easter Ross. The oil must be exploited, and the people of the area need the prosperity it will bring. But it is in everyone's interest that what has to be done should be done properly. It is important that the men who work at the yards should have decent working conditions, reasonable wages and decent places to live in. There must be enough schools, hospitals, clinics, doctors, policemen, and facilities for entertainment and recreation — everything needed by a community to thrive. It is important that the minimum of valuable farmland is swallowed up, that areas hospitable to wildlife are maintained, and disturbed as little as possible. The sea around the Cromarty Firth and the Moray Firth must be kept free of pollution.

To some extent the Cromarty Firth is a microcosm of what is happening to Scotland: a depressed region, accustomed to dealing from a position of weakness, desperate to attract jobs and income, suddenly faced with an invasion of organised international industry, intent on exploiting the natural resources of the North Sea, with the enthusiastic support of the British Government in Westminster. The prospects are exciting, the future charged with vitality and hope, but the possibilities are interlaced with a multitude of seemingly intractable problems. If the problems of the Cromarty Firth are not resolved satisfactorily, it is Scotland as a whole which will suffer.